America's Professional Highlight Resume Book

By: Allen Phillip Alexandre

A Molding Messengers Publication

America's Professional Highlight Resume Book

Copyright © 2020 by Allen Phillip Alexandre

For information about permission to reproduce selections from this book, Write to Molding Messengers, LLC 1728 NE Miami Gardens Dr, Suite #111, North Miami Beach, FL, 33179 or email Info.Staff@MoldingMessengers.com

Print ISBN: 978-0-578-77081-9

eBook ISBN: 978-0-578-77082-6

A Molding Messengers Publication

America's Professional Highlight Resume Book

By: Allen Phillip Alexandre

A Molding Messengers Publication

America's Professional Highlight Resume Book Outline

What is a resume?

A resume is a document that focuses on one's past and present experiences highlighting qualifications, job duties, positions held, accomplishments, education, and skills.

Why is a resume needed or important?

This document provides enormous opportunities toward avenues of education, starting a business, running for office or council and lastly but imperative, attaining successful employment, promotion or raise toward a desired occupation. Resumes are used to distinguish between candidates' experiences to meet the employer's requirements; whether it is owners, schools, proprietors, companies, managers, government, council).

Resume Example

Cassandra Myers
Jacksonville, Florida
(904) 439-9934
Cassandramyers@gmail.com

Professional Summary:
Compassionate medical assistant professional with 8+ years in the medical field. Extremely patient and attentive toward all patience for a positive outcome. Strong scheduling ethic as well as maintaining confidentiality within policy and procedures. Expert in understanding medical terminology and drawing blood to meet facility needs. Received employee of the month for going over and beyond on numerous occasions.

Qualifications:
- Medical Billing and Coding Certified
- Proficient in Microsoft applications PowerPoint, Word, Excel and Outlook
- CLIA, CAP, AAB, AHCA Certified and CPR Certified
- Expert in Phlebotomy, Vital Signs, Immunoassay Test, Patient Care, Semen Analysis
- Instrument Sterilization/Autoclaving and Surgical Setup
- Scheduling, Insurance Billing, Chart Filing, Supply management

Work Experience:
Medical Assistant Technician
North Florida OBGYN, Jacksonville-Florida   *12/2017-Current*
- Increased front desk efficiency by 65% by suggesting intern hires for productivity
- Provide work in lad to include venipuncture, autoclaving and scheduled diagnostic test
- Collaborate with physician, hospitals, and lab facilities to ensure quality patient care.
- Front and back office work including computer skills, electronic medical record, answering phones, filing and paperwork

- Centralized medical records systems to smoothen records retrieval procedures, decreased 50%
- Fill in at reception and coordinated insurance pre-certifications and a multi-line phone system
- Schedule and reschedule needed appointment verified by chart or doctor

Medical Assistant Technician/Laboratory Technician
Jacksonville Ctr for Reproductive Medicine, Jacksonville-Florida   *03/2014-11/2017*
- Referred and scheduled patients for specialized testing, Cesarean deliveries, induction, surgery
- Assisted physicians within office procedures such as IUD insertions and removals, colposcopies, cryo freezing, vulvar biopsies, etc.
- Examined and analyzed urine, rectal and vaginal specimens for diagnostic and therapeutic purposes
- Reduced supply delivery cost by 80% by contracting a less expensive vendor
- Delivered exceptional customer service to over 20 patients daily during their visits
- Administered medication and injection as well as prepared and collect blood, urine, and tissue specimens for laboratory testing

Customer Service Representative/Mortgage Department
Wells Fargo, Jacksonville-Florida   *04/2012-02/2014*
- Provided customer service by answering and handling any questions, concerns or comments via incoming calls or emails
- Researched and provide customers with product and service information using all available resources
- Entered new and existing customers information daily as needed
- Processed orders, forms, and applications, complete all documents and logs according to SOP
- Identified all priority issues and routed them to the appropriate resource
- Exceeded monthly goals constantly for 6 months

Professional Sales Associate
Walmart, Jacksonville-Florida   *01/2009-03/2012*
- Provided customer service by handling all comments, concerns or questions
- Operated the cash register and collect payments for merchandise purchased via cash, check or credit card
- Assisted customers with locating merchandise as needed to ensure their shopping experience was pleasurable
- Collected and filed sales records for inventory control
- Always maintained a clean and safe environment to meet company standards
- Trained 6 new employers to become successful and meet company goals

Education:
Medical Assistant Technician
Florida Career College, Jacksonville-Florida   *Completed*

Skills:

Inventory Management	Customer Orientation	Time Management
Attention to Detail	Confidentiality	Drawing Blood
Technical Oversight	Team Work	Applying Dressing
Phone Etiquette	Analytical	Medical Terminology

Resume Guidelines

- Keep it simple
- Use basic font ex. 11, 12
- Use bullets
- Make sure you meet qualifications
- Focus on accomplishments and job duties
- Print on white paper
- Proofread resume
- Be sure to identify your location
- Add a Skills section
- Make sure your resume matches the job posting
- Check for typos
- List dates carefully
- Place resume in a professional folder
- If you have a gap in employment input the date (start and end) as well as reasoning of gap. Ex. baby sitter or caregiver. Incarcerated individuals input job worked or skills acquired in prison, no need to input incarcerated or reasons for incarceration

Resume Don'ts

- Do not include personal information, such as kids or family members
- Do not label resume "Resume"
- Do not date resume
- Do not insert photographs
- Do not insert physical characteristics
- Do not include grammar school if higher education is present
- Do not input unrelated work experience
- Do not use negative words
- Do not input references
- Do not insert "I" in a resume
- Do not use fancy paper
- Do not leave gaps in history
- Do not use font over 12
- Do not use margins over 1 inch
- Do not submit a wrinkled, stained, or ripped resume
- Do not extend resume over 2 pages
- Do not input an unprofessional email address (Ex. Hotfire@yahoo.com)

Resume Building Tips

- Use OnetOnline.org to find related skills, attributes and qualification for job attainment. Using key words from this tool enhances the resume when having to go through computer resume interceptors.
- Use Google.com to search careers of choice, an outline of job duties, and to gain an insight on creating a professional summary. Also, it is important to investigate the career of choice to be sure you are a qualified candidate.
- Too add relevance is paramount within a resume
- Utilizing the space bar in the work experience, education and skills section will help with alignment.
- Use bullets for qualification, work experience and skills section
- All section titles should be bolded and underlined utilizing the tools in Word (Home Tab) Ex. **<u>Professional Summary</u>**, **<u>Qualification</u>**, **<u>Work Experience</u>**, **<u>Education</u>** and **<u>Skill</u>**.
- Utilize paragraph format single spacing (0) lining for resume.

Resume Questionnaire

The following questionnaire will assist in filling out your resume with the correct information needed to fulfill successful employment. Answering the questions will paint a vivid picture of what skills you may bring to the table as well as education, qualifications, and occupation track desired when writing your resume. This is also a checklist to be sure there is no information unexploited.

1. List your complete name, city and state currently residing in, main phone number for contact and professional email address.

   _____
   _____
   _____

2. List all employment from present to 10 years ago. *Please do not leave gaps in employment, provide explanation.*

   _____
   _____
   _____
   _____
   _____

3. List all certifications, licenses, and skills.

   _____
   _____
   _____
   _____
   _____

4. List all accomplishments and promotions received within each job worked.

_____
_____
_____
_____
_____

5. List any education from present to past.

_____
_____
_____

6. Job desired for resume.

_____
_____
_____
_____
_____
_____

Resume Header

What is a resume header?

Resume headers serve as a hub of complied information about the candidate, focusing on first and last name, residing location (city and state), professional phone contact information and professional email address.

Why is a resume header needed or important?

This section is verification for employer's purpose pertaining to identity as well as location geography for employment. The header is also used for employer accessibility to contact the candidate via phone or email. Be sure to look over all contact information for accuracy in the event of an employer follow up toward interview opportunity or job offer.

Resume Header Section Breakdown

- Double tap the top of the Word document to access the Header feature to input complied information. Once the header is entered, it will automatically populate at the top of each page for professionalism.
- Content should be centered and single spacing (0) should be used.
- Input first and last name using bold text and font can be 12 or 13 **ONLY** for your name, providing emphasis.
- Input city and state residing
- Input phone number
- Input professional email address
- Input a professional bold lining a space under the email address

Resume Header Section Examples

Johnny Smith
New York, New York
(347) 463-3454
Johnnysmith@yahoo.com

Mary McDonald
Cleveland, Ohio
(510) 213-6711
Marymcdonald12@gmail.com

Michael Carrington
Orlando, Florida
(407) 452-0085
Michaelcarrington@icloud.com

<h1>Skills</h1>

What is a skill?

A skill is the ability to do something well and with proficiency

Why is a skill needed or important?

Skills gives an outline or measurement of an individual's competency towards a particular career field. Ones abilities can determine an employer's choice when occupying a vacancy. Be sure to use skill words within the resume for increased interview opportunity.

There are two classes of skills sets looked upon when reviewing a resume: hard skills and soft skills. Refer to OnetOnline.org for occupational skill match and display.

<h2 align="center">Hard Skills</h2>

What is a hard skill?

A hard skill is a dexterity that is learned and can measured, evaluated, and defined. Hard skills often include the specific knowledge and abilities required for success in a job.

<h3 align="center">Hard Skills Examples</h3>

- Using word processors (e.g. Word)
- Using spreadsheet (e.g. Excel)
- Using database software (e.g. Access)
- Using presentation software (e.g. PowerPoint)
- Dictation
- Bookkeeping
- Accounting
- Shorthand
- Welding
- Typing/Audio typing
- Taking minutes
- Project management
- Event management
- Graphic Design
- Programming
- Editing
- The ability to operate machinery (e.g. fork lifts)
- Use of online software (e.g. Google Analytics)
- Proficiency in a foreign language
- Familiarity with particular phone languages
- Monitoring
- Organizing
- Problem solving
- Public Speaking

- Nursing

There will be a skills section at the bottom of the resume after the Education section. Be sure to have 9 or 12 hard skills available to input within this section.

Soft Skills

What is a soft skill?

Soft skills are also known as people skills or interpersonal skills. These skills tell the way you relate to and interact with other individuals. These characteristics are often personality traits, personal attributes, inherited social cues or communication abilities needed for success on a job. Furthermore, soft skills are subjective; making them harder to measure. Hiring officials frequently search for candidates with soft skills because of their ability to adapt and it being general for success.

Soft Skills Example

- Patient
- Realistic
- Hard-Working
- Thorough
- Disciplined
- Punctual
- Confident
- Creative
- Attentive
- Cheerful
- Loyal
- Dependable
- Reliable
- Quick
- Timely
- Resourceful
- Tidy
- Composed
- Perceptive
- Motivated
- Sympathetic
- Humble
- Enthusiastic
- Mature
- Assertive

Transferable Skills

What is a transferrable skill?

Transferable skills are abilities that can be taken from one employment, intern or volunteer situation to another. Knowledge acquired through personal experience such as jobs, classes, hobbies, sports, schooling etc. Essentially, it is any talent established and able to be used in future occupations. Transferrable skills are a mixture of hard and soft skills.

Transferrable Skills Example

- A transferrable skill applied to a business could consist of parenting skills in the opening of a pre-school
- Adapt to Situations: Learn a new task and/ or work in a different area with different co-workers
- Decision Making: Make good judgements about what to do in a difficult situation, even when the supervisor is not present
- Learn Quickly: Do new things and carry out new responsibilities easily by watching others or by following instructions
- Dependable: Can be counted on to do what you said you would do
- Punctual: Always on time for things
- Assemble Products: Put things together with your hands
- Pleasant: Nice person for others to talk to and be with
- Helpful: Enjoy helping people solve their problems

Top 15 hard, soft, and transferable skills for successful employment outcomes and retainment

1. Integrity/Honesty
2. Dependability/Reliability
3. Flexibility/Adaptability
4. Work Ethic
5. Customer Service
6. Team Member
7. Computer Skills
8. Knowing how to learn
9. Listening
10. Reading
11. Writing
12. Math
13. Interpersonal/Social
14. Personal Appearance/ Hygiene
15. Communication/Speaking

Qualifications

What is a qualification/requirement?

Qualifications and requirements are any learned and acquired expertise appropriate for a specific occupation. A qualification can be seen as a Hard Skill but amplified on the basis on skill set.

Why is a qualification/requirement needed or important?

Qualifications and requirements are the factors which aid the employer in determining the right client candidates often weigh heavily on meeting qualifications. These requirements drastically improve one's resume presentation levels of proficiency to carry out assigned occupational duties.

Qualification/Requirement Section Breakdown

- Input 5 to 6 qualifications
- Each bullet is detailed and focused toward meeting the employer's vacancy
- This is the section to include certifications or licenses attained for quality and growth within an occupation
- Googling the desired occupational requirements or utilizing OnetOnline.org can help in displaying which qualification fits one's skill set as well as in aid in proper verbiage
- Bullets should be used in the qualification section

Qualification/Requirement Examples

- Clinical and administrative expertise
- HIPPA as well as Medical Billing and Coding Certified
- Proficient in Microsoft applications including PowerPoint, Word, Excel and Outlook
- CLIA, CAP, AAB, AHCA Certified and CPR Certified
- Expert in Phlebotomy, Vital Signs, Immunoassay Test, Patient Care, Semen Analysis
- Instrument Sterilization/Autoclaving and Surgical Setup
- Scheduling, Insurance Billing, Chart Filing, Supply management
- Exceptional verbal and written communication skills
- Expert in project coordination supervision
- Peer Counseling and Life Builders Certification
- Knowledgeable in various theories of leadership and management
- Optimal time management and productivity
- OSHA certified implementing safety and security
- Excellent outreach, project management and link-building skills
- Resourceful and focused with strong decision making and organizational skills
- Guidance and counseling to ensure development
- Proven ability to determine answers and solutions quickly
- Track record of listening and responding to customers' needs and concerns
- Ability to express empathy as well as sympathy toward customers
- Highly skilled on providing information regarding products and services of the company
- Special talent for handling irate and angry customers
- Experience in conducting research and collect evidence appropriate to legal cases

- Strong analytical power toward data research
- Ability to work well with others on a team of attorneys, paralegals, administrative assistants, supervised by an attorney Lead Counsel
- Computer proficiency with Microsoft Office and online legal research systems West Law, Quilix and Trial Works
- Child Development Associate (CDA)-council for Professional Development.
- 45 Department of Child and Family (DCF) training hours- Childcare Development.

Accomplishments

What is an accomplishment?

An accomplishment is any achievement reached using one's skills and abilities within a specific task, duty, or occupation overall.

Why is an accomplishment needed or important?

Accomplishments can help the employer highlight strong points that can be an asset for the organization. Accomplishments also display one's will to succeed within a company which can sway employers dramatically.

Accomplishments Breakdown

- Input awards and recognition provided while employed.
- If available and applicable, include data, this increases opportunity.
- Accomplishments should be relevant to the occupation of interest.

Accomplishment Examples

- Increased customer satisfaction by ___%
- Acknowledged by receiving ___award/certification
- Increased level statistics by ___%
- Have been a part of a team that___
- Stayed under budget for ___ quarters/years
- Promoted only after ___ months on the job
- Winning a race, a league or being captain of a team
- Met deadlines on a consistent basis
- Grew customer base by ___
- Trained ___ employees/volunteer/students
- Launched ___ campaigns/services/produces
- Founded___ company/association/non-profit/club
- Gained ___ *(Insert any qualification other than education)*
- Reached ___ objectives quicker than competitors
- Long periods without absence from employment
- Improving efficiency of ___ system in the company or organization
- Employee of the month

Professional Summary

What is a Professional Summary?

A professional summary is an outline that gives the reader (the potential employer) a highlighted sketch of one's prior experiences, skills, qualifications, and accomplishment at first glance. This is the first chance for the applicant to sell themselves. Also remember to stay relevant toward the anticipated occupation when creating a professional summary.

Why is a Professional Summary needed or important?

The professional summary is vital to include in a resume considering employer review period, which at times are brief. Employers usually skim resumes at first glance, no more than 10 seconds. Most of their time is spent at the top and bottom of the resume. Professional summaries amplify the resume for quicker result and attainment towards the desired candidate.

Professional Summary Section Breakdown

- Should be between 4 to 5 sentences
- Start with soft skills to capture the employer's attention then the occupation. Ex. Compassionate, Dedicated, Knowledgeable, Virtuous, Reliable, Dependable again relevant to the occupation
- Input years of experience within desired occupation. Ex. 3+, 5+, 7+ years
- Present 2 soft skills applicable to the occupation
- Present 2 hard skills applicable to the occupation
- Present 2 qualification applicable to the occupation
- Present 1 robust accomplishment gathered from prior experience that is applicable to the occupation

Professional Summary Section Examples

1. Compassionate medical assistant professional with 8+ years in the medical field. Extremely patient and attentive toward all patience for a positive outcome. Strong scheduling ethic as well as maintaining confidentiality within policy and procedures. Expert in understanding medical terminology and drawing blood to meet facility needs. Received employee of the month for going over and beyond on numerous occasions.
2. Confident sales professional with 5+ years of automotive sales experience. The capability to engage with customers, building rapport to close on merchandise. Exemplary negotiating and price matching skills focused toward growing company revenue. Proficient written and verbal communication etiquette with knowledge of sales databases. Successfully exceeded monthly company goals 11 out of 12 months this prior year.
3. Resourceful call center professional with 10+ years of customer service experience. Maintains a high level of composure and empathy to minimize customer dissatisfaction, increasing customer loyalty. Proven capacity to troubleshoot issues equating time management. Strong product knowledge as well as computer efficiency. Customer Service certificate provided for 95% satisfaction rate met.
4. Well-equipped professional specialist with 3+ years of customer service experience. Extremely open minded to new ideas as well as concepts. Strong ability to learn new tasks quickly and proficiently. Goal oriented individual dedicated to high levels of

customer satisfaction and meeting aggressive goals. Successfully maintained a 90% retention rates.

5. Dedicated professional faculty member with 14+ years teaching and facilitating experience. Excellent communication skills as well as organized and driven with the innate ability to stay on task. Uses effective and efficient methods for meeting organization and people needs on different metric levels. Documented success in leadership, teaching, training, Microsoft applications and technical operations. Awarded teacher of the year 7 times.

Work Experience

What is work experience?

Work experience is any position held prior to current job duties, skills, abilities and accomplishments attained over a period of employment. Work experience can vary in careers but also directed toward a specific career.

Why is work experience needed or important?

Work experience gained from previous employment helps the employer gauge the level on understanding as well as environmental adaptation the candidate may present. This section displays detailed job duties administered on a daily basis that may be an asset to the employer reviewing the resume. It is imperative to match the desired occupational duties increasing possibilities of being selected for hire.

Work Experience Section Breakdown

- It is imperative to input all latest work experience to earliest and extend 10 years but 7 at minimum
- Input position held
- Input company name, city, and state (Be sure to italicize this text)
- Include dates worked for employer from beginning to end. (Be sure to italicize this text)
- Bullets should be used when adding each job duty
- Input job duties relevant to the desired job
- Remember do not leave gaps in employment and be sure to provide valid reasoning. Volunteering, care giving, at home parenting can also be seen as activities where duties are performed that equates work experience
- Be sure to provide detailed reasoning of each job duty. Ex. Met with patients to conduct face-to-face screening assessments to determine eligibility
- Provide 4-6 job duties
- Input 1 (2 accomplishments preferably) for each job. Do not be afraid to use percentages and numbers to strengthen this section
- Be sure to use correct present and past tense when formulating each job duty
- If you have been promoted within an organization, one work experience can be documented instead on multiple employment sections. Ex. Crew member promoted to Team lead crew member; Assistant Manager promoted to General Manager
- Using Google or OnetOnline.org to seek the desired occupational job duties that can help in displaying which qualification fits one's skill set as well as in aid in prior verbiage

Work Experience Section Example

Office Manager
Enterprise Global, Jacksonville-Florida   *01/2009-08/2016*
- Partnered with HR to maintain office policies, as necessary
- Organized office operations and procedures and coordinated with IT department on all office equipment
- Managed relationships with vendors, service providers and landlord, ensuring that all items are invoiced and paid on time
- Managed contracts and conducted price negotiations with office vendors, service providers and office leases
- Ensured results are measured against standards, while making necessary changes along the way
- Researched and contracted vendor office supplies to reduce item expenses by 15%
- Developed digital file structure and organized scanning of existing document files

Mail Clerk
Internal Service, Atlanta-Georgia   *06/2015-Present*
- Weigh individual bags or pieces of mail scales, postage of computer on basis of weight
- Accurately filed and delivered mail to all company departments
- Coordinate delivery of large projects with mailroom clerk
- Lift heavy bins on a daily basis to sort mail as needed in the required area
- Sort and route incoming mail and collect outgoing mail, using carts as necessary
- Accept and check containers of mail from large volume mailers, couriers and contractors
- Won the XWD "Employee of the year award" for extraordinary service and dedication

Patient Care Secretary
Vitas Healthcare, New York-New York   *01/2016- 06/2018*
- Establishes, maintains, and closes patient charts in an orderly manner
- Handles all patient care data entry and performs receptionist duties as required
- Assure for compliance with local, state and federal laws, medical regulations and established company policies and procedures
- Participate in staff meetings, department meetings, team meetings as well as briefings
- Answer phones for receptionist during lunch and breaks or during absence
- Aided in growth within the practice from 100-250 in a 3-month span
- Successfully managed the concerns of 500+ patients

Sales Representative promoted to Manager
American Auto Rental and Sales, Jasper-Florida   *03/1995-11/2013*
- Created, implemented and managed a high impact outside sales plan to capitalize on current and new business opportunity
- Developed strong sales culture within branch to capitalize on additional revenue
- Consistently was top third of customer service index

- Contacted new and existing accounts to discuss service and procedures ensuring top customer
service
- Effectively communicated with employees to maintain clear and defined personal expectations
- Meet aggressive and exceeded yearly company goals increasing company revenue
- Ranked number 1 Managers for the region on a consistent basis

Lead Toddler Teacher/Floater
Little Britches Learning Center, Houston-Texas   *10/2009-01/2017*
- Conducted group and individual classroom activities with students based on differentiated
learning needs to ensure all students are learning at full potential
- Organized parent teacher conference to maximize student learning opportunities
- Employed assessment tools and proactive strategies to improve instruction methods
- Held team meeting informing teacher of new policies, resolving team conflicts and handling
customer complaints
- Facilitated activities that developed students physical, emotional and social growth
- Communicated to parents through parent boards, daily sheets, pictures of classroom activities,
emails, newsletters and through verbal communication
- Provided Potty training, diaper changing, creating lesson plans, following a curriculum, coached
by Children's Episcopal Services and manage the classroom

Caretaker
Private, St. Louis-Tennessee   *04/2015-Present*
- Performed housekeeping task such as cleaning, washing and vacuuming
- Assisted in daily living activities such as grooming, organizing and prioritizing
- Provided engagement for direction and understanding as well as monitored daily activities
- Prepared daily task and instructions for completion as well as preformed money management
- Scheduled appointments on an as needed basis to maintain health and environment
- Improved personal health and self-efficiency within a 12-month period
- Stayed under budget for 4 years, increasing profits

Education

What is education in terms of a resume?

Education is a tool that is learned within a specific occupation used to carry out job duties at different employment levels to meet positive organizational outcomes or goals.

Why is education important or needed?

Education helps the employer match different levels of expertise between candidates to choose the one most fit for the vacant position. The more education the higher the possibilities of getting the desired job.

Education Section Breakdown

- Input education from earliest to latest completed
- Be sure education is relevant to desired position
- Input any school graduated or currently attending
- Input any degrees obtained, include major and minor if applicable
- Input city and state degree received
- School education received along with city, state and completion status should be italicized
- Input high school only if it is the only education achieved at the present time
- Input Completed or Current for education. Dates completed are not needed, this can wait until the interview
- Input education from Universities, Colleges, Trade and Vocational schools

Education Section Examples

Medical Assistant Technician
Florida Career College, Jacksonville-Florida   *Completed*

-

High School Diploma
North Miami Beach Senior, North Miami Beach-Florida   *Completed*

-

Juris Doctor Candidate
Florida Agriculture and Metropolitan University College of Law,
 Orlando-Florida   *Current*

-

Master of Business Administration
Florida Institute of Technology, Melbourne-Florida   *Completed*

-

Bachelor of Arts Political Science/ Pre-Law Program
University of North Florida, Jacksonville-Florida   *Completed*

Business Administration
Florida State College of Jacksonville- Florida   *Current*

-

Medical Billing and Coding Certification (CCS)
Florida Metropolitan University, Jacksonville-Florida   *Completed*

-

Andrew Jackson High
Jacksonville-Florida   *Completed*

-

Master of Arts Degree in Human Resources Management
Webster University, St. Louis - Missouri   *Completed*

-

Bachelor of Science Degree in Fisheries Biology
University of Arkansas at Pine Bluff, Pine Bluff – Arkansas   *Completed*

Skills Section Breakdown

Skills wills always be the last section of the resume to continue to catch the employer's interest. Only input hard skills displaying additional abilities to increase employment outcomes. As stated in the skills section on page 2 (9 or 12 skills should be inputted). Again, be sure to stay relevant to the desired position.

Skills Section Examples

Medical Assistant

Inventory Management	Customer Orientation	Time Management
Attention to Detail	Confidentiality	Drawing Blood
Technical Oversight	Team Work	Applying Dressing
Phone Etiquette	Analytical	Med. Terminology

Call Center Customer Service

Analytical Expressive	Communication	Strong Composure
Team Building	Customer Oriented	Time Management
Negotiation	Problem Solving	Computer Navigation
Attention to Detail	Confidentiality	Empathy

Counselor

Crisis Prevention Intervention	Community Resource	Clinical Documentation
Group Intervention	Report Writing	Guidance and Counsel
Case Management	Substance Abuse	Facility Management
Problem Solving	Strategic Planning	Communication

Litigation Law

Court Procedures	Legal Writing	Decisive
Project Management	Calm Under Pressure	Writing Transcripts
Research and Analysis	Effective Multitasking	Creative Problem Solving
Goal-Oriented	Client Profiles	Inquisitive

Teacher

Instructing Social	Perceptiveness	Learning Strategies
Active Listening	Coordination	Time Management
Writing Comprehension	Reading Comprehension	Public Speaking
Problem Solving	Technical Oversight	Group Orientation

Animal Caretaker

Exhibit Educator	Animal Nutrition	Service Oriented
Animal Grooming Tools	Animal Rapport	Technical Oversight
Kettle Cleaning	Exotic & Domestic Animals	Animal Handling

Retail Sales Professional

Risk Management	Cash Supervision	Business Development
Budget	Management Sales and Advertising	Merchandising Techniques
Procurement	Policies Implementation	Inventory/Expense Control

Resume Template

Header: First Name and Last Name
Residing City and State
Main phone number
Professional email

Professional Summary: 4 to 5 sentences. One's occupation, 2 soft skills, 2 hard skills, 2 qualifications, 1 accomplishment. Stay relevant to desired job.

_____
_____
_____
_____

Qualifications: 5 to 6 requirements. Stay relevant to desired job.

- _____
- _____
- _____
- _____
- _____
- _____

Work Experience: Position held, company name, city and state as well as month and date worked for employer. 4 to 6 job duties (10 years preferably), 1 to 2 occupational accomplishments. Repeat process for each job. Stay relevant to desired job. **Tip for margins- Utilize space bar and single spacing (0).**
Position Held: _____

Company Name: _____, City____ -State____   Date started: __/__ -Date Ended: __/__

- _____
- _____
- _____
- _____
- _____
- _____

Education: College, Trade School, Vocational School, Certification Schooling and apply High School ONLY if there is no other educational record. Repeat. **Tip for margins- Utilize space bar and Single spacing (0).**
Degree_____

School, College or University_____, City____-State____   Status Completed or Current

Skills: Apply 9 to 12 hard skills ONLY. **Tip for margins- Utilize space bar and single spacing (0).**

Resume Example

Richard Mathews
Jacksonville, Florida
(904) 329-3920
Richardmatthews@gmail.com

Professional Summary:
Mental Health Professional/Rehabilitation Counselor with 7+ years of solid understanding in recovery, supervision, peer mentoring and mental health. Adept knowledge in counseling practices offering a supportive approach in the form of guidance, empathy and education. Excellent ability to use live experience and motivational interviewing techniques when navigating through different stages of change. Successfully rehabilitated over 100 clients through guidance, counseling and resourcing.

Qualifications:
- Division of Vocational Rehabilitation Certificate completion (Adult and Juveniles)
- Behavioral Science Concentration completion
- Improving Lives, Improving Communities Certificate
- Baker Act Basics, The Florida Certification Board completion
- Demonstrates knowledge of DSM-IV and DSM-V
- Excellent outreach, project management and link-building skills

Work Experience:
Research Assessment Specialist
Florida State University, Jacksonville-Florida   *06/2018-Present*
- Confer with participants to explain purpose of study and obtain informed consent; administer computer assisted personal interviews of behavioral health measures and clinical assessments
both within and outside of state prisons
- Collaborate with families and professional advocates to ensure guidance and success
- Closely track and maintain contact with study participants once they are released from prison,
to ensure that follow-up interviews can be completed
- Ensure compliance with protocol guidelines and requirements of the Florida State University Institutional Review Board successfully and consistently
- Identify problems and/or inconsistencies with data collection; and monitor study participant's progress to include documentation and reporting of adverse events

Chief Operations Officer/Employment Counselor
Prestige Workforce, Jacksonville-Florida   *07/2017-06/2018*
- Performed career counseling and rehabilitation, advocate on the behalf of clients
- Extended special guidance to clients with disabilities and ensure they are provided with the favorable work environment suiting their unique requirements
- Interviewed and assessed clients, obtaining information to formulate an appropriate plan to implement for rehabilitation and independence
- Followed-up with clients at appropriate intervals to assess program and record outcomes

- Conducted groups of between 10-20 clients on a weekly basis discussing rehabilitation
- Created and implemented curriculums for training and career exploration

Vocational Rehabilitation Counselor/Job Developer
Service Source, Jacksonville-Florida   *04/2015-06/2017*
- Familiarized self with all medications prescribed to clients and educates them about the medication benefits and potential side effects
- Reviewed and responded to electronic and hand-written mail, memoranda and other correspondence and responds to phone inquiries timely (within 24-hours or next available business day) in a professional manner
- Maintained ongoing chart audit to ensure compliance and quality assurance of services provide
- Demonstrated proficiency in utilizing resources as supportive services and discharge planning
- Served as a liaison for the client, family, referral source and other social service agencies
- Vocational Rehabilitation award MOPS (Making Other People Successful)
- Worked effectively with culturally diverse groups and individuals experiencing an exacerbation of either psychiatric, substance use and/or medical symptoms, as well as experiencing a stressful situation

Staff Mentor/Supervisor
Miami Youth Academy Substance Abuse Facility, Miami-Florida   *02/2014-01/2015*
- Met with patients to conduct face-to-face screening assessments to determine eligibility
- Evaluated patient issues and needs then reporting them to clinical team for treatment plans
- Prioritized needs and problems related to patient orientation
- Supervised facility and staff on a daily basis, providing reports and outcomes
- Proficiency in utilizing community resources as supportive services and discharge/aftercare planning as evidenced by a fully completed and accurate Aftercare Plan
- Created operational facility structure and scheduling

Juvenile Detention Officer II
Florida Department of Juvenile Justice, Miami-Florida   *06/2011-01/2014*
- Provided assistance or personal care to mental health and substance abuse disorders
- Monitored and reviewed all incoming medical, criminal, psychological data, and reports
- Communicated with outside resources to obtain relative information
- Considered all psychological definitions and treatments while diagnosing young teenagers
- Used medical, criminal, and psychological reports and data to govern future decisions
- Promoted from Officer I to Officer II within 6 months of employment

Education:

Master's in Behavioral Science	Nova Southeastern University	Completed
Public Safety Certification	Broward College	Completed
Bachelor's in Criminal Justice	Edward Waters College	Completed

Skills:

Crisis Prevention Intervention	Community Resource	Clinical Documentation
Group Intervention	Report Writing	Guidance and Counseling
Case Management	Substance Abuse	Facility Management
Problem Solving	Strategic Planning	Communication

www.ingramcontent.com/pod-product-compliance
Lightning Source LLC
Chambersburg PA
CBHW081750200326
41597CB00024B/4455